DA

1

STUDY OBEDIENCE.

❑ Obedience is simply doing exactly what God instructs. It will require discipline, total focus and determination.

❑ Obedience is the only thing God has ever required of man. That's why your smallest act of obedience is documented and celebrated by God.

❑ Anything you give *attention* to, you will do well. So, find what makes God happy... and do it.

DAY
2

REMEMBER, OBEDIENCE BEGINS AT WAKE-UP.

❑ Begin this day with prayer. Ask yourself. "Is my schedule for today truly the agenda God has chosen for me?" If not, *change it.*

❑ Yesterday is in the *tomb.* Tomorrow is in the *womb.* The most important day of your life is *today.*

❑ Concentrate on walking in total obedience for the next 24 hours. Keep your ear next to the mouth of God *every single hour.*

WISDOM FROM THE WORD

"My voice shalt thou hear in the morning, O Lord; in the morning will I direct my prayer unto thee, and will look up."
Psalms 5:3

DAY
3

GET TO KNOW GOD'S VOICE.

❑ God talks... more than anyone you will ever meet. He talks *as often as you need help.*

❑ I cannot explain to you my mother's voice. You would have to spend time with my mother.

❑ I cannot explain to you my Heavenly Father's voice. You will have to spend *time* with Him to know His *voice. Obedience is impossible unless you discern His voice.*

WISDOM FROM THE WORD

"My sheep hear My voice,
and I know them, and they follow Me:"
John 10:27

DAY
4

SCHEDULE INTIMATE MOMENTS WITH GOD

❑ You make appointments with your doctor, your lawyer, your boss. Why not schedule a one-hour appointment daily with God?

❑ Do it every day *at the same time.* This helps create rhythm in your life.

❑ *You* will *hear* what you have never heard before. You will *discover* what you have never known before. You will *become* what you have always wanted to become.

WISDOM FROM THE WORD

"...He went into his house; and his windows being open in his chamber toward Jerusalem, he kneeled upon his knees three times a day, and prayed, and gave thanks before his God, as he did aforetime."
Daniel 6:10

DAY
5

RECOGNIZE MESSENGERS FROM GOD.

❏ When Satan wants to *destroy* you, he sends a *person*. When God wants to *bless* you, He sends a *person*.

❏ *Recognize them.* Whether they are packaged like a John the Baptist in a loincloth of camel's hair, or the silk robes of King Solomon.

❏ Your reaction to a man or woman of God is carefully documented by God. When God talks to you, it is often through spiritual leaders in your life. *Don't ignore them.*

WISDOM FROM THE WORD

"He that receiveth a prophet in the name of a prophet shall receive a prophet's reward; and he that receiveth a righteous man in the name of a righteous man shall receive a righteous man's reward."
Matthew 10:41

DAY
6

FACE YOUR SINS HONESTLY.

☐ Everyone has sinned against God. Publicly or privately.

☐ You are instructed in the Word to confess that sin and turn away from it. Do it now. *Obey Him.*

☐ Only a fool would attempt to deceive God. Your confession will unlock His mercy.

WISDOM FROM THE WORD

"He that covereth his sins shall not prosper: but whoso confesseth and forsaketh them shall have mercy."
Proverbs 28:13

DAY
7

RUN TOWARD GOD.

❑ *Things happen in the presence of God that do not happen anywhere else.*

❑ When you get in His presence, you *think* differently. You *talk* differently. You *act* differently. Your *best* comes out of you.

❑ So get started today. Like any damaged product, we must *return* to our manufacturer for repair.

WISDOM FROM THE WORD

"All that the Father giveth me shall come to Me; and him that cometh to me I will in no wise cast out."
John 6:37

DAY
8

OBEY YOUR PARENTS.

❑ *Your reaction toward your parents influences God's reaction towards you.*

❑ In the Ten Commandments, the commandment to honor your parents was the first to be followed by a promise.

❑ Carefully consider any advice your parents give you. *Honor* it. Contribute to their life. Take their opinions seriously. It will be forever written on the mind of God.

WISDOM FROM THE WORD

"Children, obey your parents in the Lord: For this is right."
Ephesians 6:1

DAY
9

OBEY YOUR BOSS.

❑ Bosses are not always easy to please. They may sometimes be like sandpaper God is using to polish the rough edges of your life.

❑ It is awesome that the Creator of this universe stopped long enough to personally advise *employees*... to be obedient to their *employers*.

❑ Obedience in the workplace consists of *careful listening, taking notes and total concentration on completion of a task.* Do it. God will prosper you for it.

WISDOM FROM THE WORD

"Servants, be obedient to them that are your masters according to the flesh, with fear and trembling, in singleness of your heart, as unto Christ;"
Ephesians 6:5

DAY
10

LEARN TO LISTEN.

❏ *Somebody knows something you do not know.* That information may be invaluable. You have to *listen* to receive it.

❏ Something inside you may want to scream out for attention. You have a longing to be heard. Restrain yourself. *Learn to listen.*

❏ Remember, God talks. How often? *As often as you need help.*

WISDOM FROM THE WORD

*"A wise man will hear,
and will increase learning;
and a man of understanding shall
attain unto wise counsels:"*

Proverbs 1:5

DAY
11

DESPISE DISOBEDIENCE.

☐ You must develop a hatred for evil. *You can only conquer what you hate.*

☐ Take a moment to note that millions of babies are murdered by *abortion.* Thousands have splattered their blood on our highways because of *alcoholism.* Thousands more are destroyed through *drugs.* All of these are *results of disobedience.*

☐ Determine to obey. *Walk toward God.* Toward righteousness. You will never regret it.

WISDOM FROM THE WORD

"The fear of the Lord is to hate evil..."
Proverbs 8:13a

DAY
12

FEAR GOD.

❑ Fearing God is not necessarily being afraid of Him. It means to honor Him and have a healthy respect for His opinions, instructions, and plans.

❑ What you respect will *come toward* you. What you do not respect will *move away* from you.

❑ God honors those who fear Him. Attending His house on the Lord's day, tithing and morning prayer are signals to Him that He matters to you.

WISDOM FROM THE WORD

"Let us hear the conclusion of the whole matter: Fear God, and keep His commandments: for this is the whole duty of man. For God shall bring every work into judgment, with every secret thing, whether it be good, or whether it be evil."

Ecclesiastes 12:13, 14

DAY
13

EXAMINE THE REWARDS OF OBEDIENCE.

❑ Obedience is doing whatever God instructs you to do. *Each instruction is linked to a miracle in your future.*

❑ *Each act of obedience shortens the distance to any miracle you are pursuing.*

❑ Remember, God only feels obligated to the *obedient. The obedient always receive answers to their prayers.*

WISDOM FROM THE WORD

"And whatsoever we ask, we receive of Him, because we keep His commandments, and do those things that are pleasing in His sight."
I John 3:22

DAY
14

CONSIDER THE CONSEQUENCES OF YOUR REBELLION.

❑ Rebellion is punished. *Always.* It may not happen today, but it is inevitable. Each Seed of disobedience is like a magnet attracting tragedies into your life.

❑ *God will never advance you beyond your last act of disobedience.* Joshua learned this at the Battle of Ai, when Achan attempted a cover-up of his sin. The Israelites lost the battle.

❑ God is not stupid. He is not blind. He sees everything. Sooner or later... He reacts to it. *You cannot afford the losses your rebellion will create.*

WISDOM FROM THE WORD

"Then shall they call upon Me, but I will not answer; they shall seek Me early, but they shall not find Me: For that they hated knowledge, and did not choose the fear of the Lord: They would none of my counsel: they despised all my reproof Therefore shall they eat of the fruit of their own way, and be filled with their own devices."

Proverbs 1:28-31

DAY
15

APPRECIATE ORDER.

❑ Order is *the accurate arrangement of things*. Your car is parked in your garage. Your clothes hang *orderly* in your closet.

❑ When you increase order (the accurate arrangement of people and events) you increase *productivity*. Plan your day carefully.

❑ Unplanned hours will always gravitate toward your weakness. Unplanned days are unproductive days. *Unplanned days are incubators for your greatest mistakes.*

WISDOM FROM THE WORD

"Let all things be done decently and in order."
I Corinthians 14:40

DAY
16

PRAY OVER EVERY DECISION.

❑ *Something happens when you pray that would not have happened had you not prayed.*

❑ Every decision you make is a turning point in your life. Making the right decision determines whether you succeed or fail.

❑ Prayer is the proof that you respect God. It is a sign that you recognize His power to change your circumstances. It attracts God. *Do it.*

WISDOM FROM THE WORD

"...The effectual fervent prayer of a righteous man availeth much."
James 5:16b

DAY
17

HONOR THE CHAIN OF YOUR AUTHORITY.

❏ Imagine a nation without a leader. A workplace without a boss. An army without a general. *Authority creates order.*

❏ God created the chain of authority. The pastor that *oversees* his congregation. The father that *rules* his home. The employer who *supervises* his staff.

❏ *Honor the chain of authority in your life.* Joseph did. David did. It is the *hidden secret* to promotion.

WISDOM FROM THE WORD

"Obey them that have the rule over you, and submit yourselves:"
Hebrews 13:17a

DAY
18

EXPECT BLESSINGS.

☐ You have listened. You have heard. You have obeyed the instructions of God. Now, *expect miracles.*

☐ Blessings are benefits from God that increase your joy, and enable you to complete His instructions for your life. They are promised only to the *obedient.*

☐ Obedience is *always* rewarded. Blessings are guaranteed to "those who walk uprightly." *Obedience is the only real proof of your faith in God.*

WISDOM FROM THE WORD

"And all these blessings shall come on thee, and overtake thee, if thou shalt hearken unto the voice of the Lord thy God." Deuteronomy 28:2

"...No good thing will he withhold from them that walk uprightly."
Psalms 84:11b

OBEDIENCE

DAY
19

PLAN ON SUPERNATURAL PROTECTION.

❏ Every day of your life, Satan will make attempts to destroy you. The story of Job illustrates this.

❏ You are not capable of totally protecting yourself. You will require *supernatural* interventions.

❏ Plan on supernatural protection *daily*. It is one of your rewards for hourly *obedience*.

WISDOM FROM THE WORD

*"But if thou shalt indeed obey His voice,
and do all that I speak;
then I will be an enemy unto thine
enemies and an adversary
unto thine adversaries."*
Exodus 23:22

DAY
20

COMMAND SICKNESS TO LEAVE.

☐ God wants you well. He wants you healthy in your body, mind and spirit.

☐ In the Old Testament, He gave Israel dietary laws regarding foods they were to avoid. *Disobedience* brought *sickness.* *Obedience* brought *health.*

☐ Obey God *today.* Then command sickness and disease to depart from you and your household, in the Name of Jesus.

WISDOM FROM THE WORD

"And ye shall serve the Lord your God, and He shall bless thy bread, and thy water; and I will take sickness away from the midst of thee."
Exodus 23:25

DAY
21

LOOK AT LOSERS AND LEARN.

❏ When you see an alcoholic or drug addict, you see someone who has lost the most precious things in life - his health, loving relationships, and self-confidence.

❏ God promises *gain* to the obedient. He guarantees loss to the disobedient.

❏ Every loser can be a lesson to us. LEARN.

WISDOM FROM THE WORD

"There is a way which seemeth right unto a man, but the end thereof are the ways of death."
Proverbs 14:12

DAY
22

STUDY CHAMPIONS

- ❑ David was a champion. Samuel was a champion. *They walketh the path of obedience.*

- ❑ Learn from their mistakes, their successes, their lives. Losers build their lives around their *weaknesses*. Champions build their lives around their *strengths*.

- ❑ You are destined for greatness, too. *Talk* it. Believe it. Live it. Champions simply use the *Master Key* of obedience.

WISDOM FROM THE WORD

"And what shall I more say? for the time would fail me to tell of Gedeon, and of Barak, and of Samson, and of Jephthae; of David also, and Samuel, and of the prophets; Who through faith subdued kingdoms, wrought righteousness, obtained promises, stopped the mouths of lions, Quenched the violence of fire, escaped the edge of the sword, out of weakness were made strong, waxed valiant in fight, turned to flight the armies of the aliens." Hebrews 11:32-34

DAY
23

DISCERN GOD'S DAILY AGENDA.

❏ Your agenda (schedule for today) should be decided in the *presence of God.* Your daily agenda will create miracles or tragedies depending on whether or not you are led by the spirit of God *HOURLY.*

❏ *Obedience is an hourly event.*

❏ Your inner peace is a *signal.* Don't make a phone call, an appointment or a decision *unless you are at peace* in your heart about it.

WISDOM FROM THE WORD

"For as many as are led by the Spirit of God, they are the sons of God."
Romans 8:14

DAY
24

ENDURE CORRECTION.

❑ *Wisdom begins with correction.* Errors must be exposed. Mistakes must be admitted.

❑ Think back over your life. Think of the person who taught you the most. He was probably the one who *corrected* you the most.

❑ Hell is full of people who *rejected* correction. Heaven is full of people who *accepted* it.

WISDOM FROM THE WORD

"For whom the Lord loveth He chasteneth, and scourgeth every son whom He receiveth. Now no chastening for the present seemeth to be joyous, but grievous: Nevertheless afterward it yieldeth the peaceable fruit of righteousness unto them which are exercised thereby."
Hebrews 12:6,11

DAY
25

DEMAND OBEDIENCE FROM YOUR CHILDREN.

❑ Your children are gifts from the Lord. Take time to unlock their greatness. Help create *order* in their lives.

❑ Make a list of their daily chores. They deserve to know your *specific expectations* of them.

❑ *Penalize them* for disobedience. *Reward them* for obedience. Do it consistently. They are worth the time and effort.

WISDOM FROM THE WORD

"Chasten thy son while there is hope, and let not thy soul spare for his crying."
Proverbs 19:18

DAY
26

ESCAPE THE CURSE

❑ Tithe means "tenth." The Bible indicates ten percent of your income belongs to God.

❑ This tithe is "Holy Seed." Each time you receive your paycheck, give ten percent back to God, like a Seed that a farmer sows to create a crop. Then, *expect a harvest.*

❑ Millions live under a curse. They have hoarded the tithes for themselves. Whatever you do, obey God in your giving. *Escape the curse.*

WISDOM FROM THE WORD

"Will a man rob God? yet ye have robbed Me. But ye say, Wherein have we robbed thee? In tithes and offerings. Ye are cursed with a curse: for ye have robbed Me, even this whole nation. Bring ye all the tithes into the storehouse, that there may be meat in Mine house, and prove Me now herewith, saith the Lord of hosts, if I will not open you the windows of heaven, and pour you out a blessing, that there shall not be room enough to receive it. Malachi 3:8-10

DAY
27

DON'T RUN FROM YOUR CALLING.

▌ You may be called to the Ministry. *Don't fight it.* Thousands rebel every day against the call of God into the ministry. Satan wreaks havoc with their life because of it.

▌ Think back. See if you can remember any moment God spoke to your heart to become a pastor, an evangelist, a missionary. *Consider it again.*

▌ *Are you called?* In Jesus Name, find a man of God who will mentor you and unlock this eternal anointing upon your life. You will *never be happy anywhere else.*

WISDOM FROM THE WORD

"...Go ye into all the world, and preach the gospel to every creature."
Mark 16:15
"Before I formed thee in the belly I knew thee; and before thou camest forth out of the womb I sanctified thee, and I ordained thee a prophet unto the nations." Jeremiah 1:5

DAY
28

DISCERN YOUR ASSIGNMENT.

☐ When God created you, He gave you certain gifts and talents *to accomplish something He wanted you to do.* We call that *"an assignment."*

☐ *The problem that infuriates you the most is often the problem God has assigned you to solve.*

☐ *Everything God creates is a solution to something.* You are a lifejacket to someone drowning. Find them. *Those who unlock your compassion are those to whom you have been assigned.*

WISDOM FROM THE WORD

"I will praiseThee; for I am fearfully and wonderfully made: marvellous are Thy works; and that my soul knoweth right well."
Psalm 139:14

OBEDIENCE

DAY
29

NEVER STAY WHERE GOD HAS NOT ASSIGNED YOU.

❏ You are *geographically* designed. This means that your nationality, your race, sex and even where you were born was decided by God.

❏ You are *geographically* assigned. This means there is a place, a city, a location where God wants you. *There... is where you will flourish and succeed.*

❏ Elijah was *sent* to the brook. There he was *reassigned* to the widow of Zarephath. *Each instruction from God is linked to your assignment.* Your financial provisions are usually *waiting* for you at *the place where God has assigned you.*

WISDOM FROM THE WORD

"And the word of the Lord came unto him, saying, Get thee hence, and turn thee eastward, and hide thyself by the brook Cherith... And the word of the Lord came unto him, saying, Arise, get thee to Zarephath, which belongeth to Zidon, and dwell there:" I Kings 17:2, 3, 8, 9a

DAY
30

DO SOMETHING RIGHT TODAY.

❑ It is *easy* to impress God. Just do something *right*. Follow His instructions. Those instructions may come through His Word, the inner voice of the Holy Spirit, or through men of God in your life.

❑ Attend church *faithfully*. Tithe *consistently*. Pray *daily*. Read the Bible *habitually*. Witness to someone about Jesus.

❑ Those little golden hinges swing huge doors to miracles. Get started... NOW. Humble yourself. *Reach. You will succeed.*

WISDOM FROM THE WORD

"If my people, which are called by My Name, shall humble themselves, and pray, and seek My face, and turn from their wicked ways; then will I hear from heaven, and will forgive their sin, and will heal their land."
II Chronicles 7:14

DAY
31

RETURN FOR REPAIR.

❏ When you receive a product you have ordered through the mail, it may arrive damaged. You have to return it to the manufacturer for repair.

❏ Your life is the same way. Sometimes the painful experiences have left us damaged. Only God can truly repair us.

❏ *Don't be afraid of God.* Dare to reach for Him. He loves you far more than you will ever know.

WISDOM FROM THE WORD

"Come now, and let us reason together, saith the Lord: though your sins be as scarlet, they shall be as white as snow; though they be red like crimson, they shall be as wool."
Isaiah 1:18

Decision Page

Will You Accept Jesus As Savior Of Your Life Today?

The Bible says, "That if thou shalt confess with thy mouth the Lord Jesus, and shall believe in thine heart that God hath raised Him from the dead, thou shalt be saved. For with the heart man believeth unto righteousness; and with the mouth confession is made unto salvation."(Rom. 10:9-10)

To receive Jesus Christ as Lord and Savior of your life, please pray this prayer from your heart today!

"Dear Jesus, I believe that you died for me and rose again on the third day. I confess I am a sinner. I need Your love and forgiveness. Come into my life, forgive my sins, and give me eternal life. I confess You now as my Lord. Thank You for my salvation, Your peace and joy. Amen."

Return This Today!

❏ Yes, Mike! I made a decision to accept Christ as my personal Savior today. Please send me my free gift copy of your book "31 Keys To A New Beginning" to help me with my new life in Christ. (B48)

"Sow A Seed Of Wisdom Into The Lives Of Those You Love!"

Here is your opportunity to invest in the lives of your Love Circle. Purchase copies of *Seeds of Wisdom On Obedience* for only $5 for 2 special people in your life. These dynamic daily devotionals are your answer to the "Daily Bread" of the Wisdom of God.

❏ Yes, Mike, I want to Sow 2 *Seeds of Wisdom On Obedience* into 2 people that I love. I have enclosed $5 for the 2 books. Please rush them immediately. (SOW088)

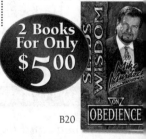

2 Books For Only $5.00

B20

Send A Self-Addressed Envelope With Check Or Money Order To: Mike Murdock P.O. Box 99 • Dallas, TX • 75221